Copyright © 2025 by Educate Learners

Published by Educate Learners

All rights reserved. No part of this publication may be reproduced, distributed, or transmitted in any form or by any means, including photocopying, recording, or other electronic or mechanical methods, without the prior written permission of the publisher, except in the case of brief quotations embodied in critical reviews and certain other noncommercial uses permitted by copyright law.

First Printing, 2025.

ISBN: 978-1-951573-58-4

www.educatelearners.com

**is for airplane, apple and alligator.**

is for bear, banana and balloon.

**C** is for cat, cupcake and chair.

is for door, donut and dinosaur.

**is for earmuffs, elephant and envelope.**

is for **flower**,
**fox**, **fence** and **fries**.

**is for grapes, giraffe and glasses.**

is for **helicopter**, hippo, heart and hat.

**is for ice cream, igloo and ice.**

is for jelly beans, jelly fish and jacks.

is for kangaroo, koala and kite.

**is for ladybug, lemon, leaves and lizard.**

is for monkey, mouse and mittens.

**is for necklace, nuts and narwhal.**

is for orange, oyster and octopus.

**is for palm tree, panda and popcorn.**

is for queen, quail and quince.

is for **roller skates**, racoon, racket and rainbow.

**is for soccer ball, seal and sun.**

**is for truck, turtle and tree.**

is for umbrella, ukulele and unicycle.

is for **volleyball**, vulture and **vegetables**.

is for **watermelon,
web** and **whale.**

is for x-ray and xylophone.

is for yak, yo-yo and yarn.

**is for zucchini, zebra and zipper.**

# Thank you for reading!

Get a free year long subscription to our online education resource library when you purchase any one of our books.

**Code: EDBOOKS**

educatelearners.com

www.ingramcontent.com/pod-product-compliance
Lightning Source LLC
Chambersburg PA
CBHW041602070526
44586CB00003BA/58